# The Xenophobe's® Guide to The Swiss

## Paul Bilton

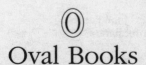

# Oval Books

Published by Oval Books
335 Kennington Road
London SE11 4QE
United Kingdom

Telephone: +44 (0)20 7582 7123
Fax: +44 (0)20 7582 1022
E-mail: info@ovalbooks.com
Web site: www.ovalbooks.com

First published by Ravette Publishing, 1995
Reprinted 1996,1997,1998

First published by Oval Books, 1999
Reprinted 2000
Revised & updated 2001
Reprinted 2003

Editor – Catriona Tulloch Scott
Series Editor – Anne Tauté

Cover designer – Jim Wire, Quantum
Printer – Cox & Wyman Ltd
Producer – Oval Projects Ltd


Xenophobe's® is a Registered Trademark.


Cover: Old Switzerland chocolate ingots and
coins are reproduced by kind permission of
Goldkenn Switzerland.


Thanks are given to John Purnell
for his help and information.


ISBN: 1-902825-45-4

# Contents

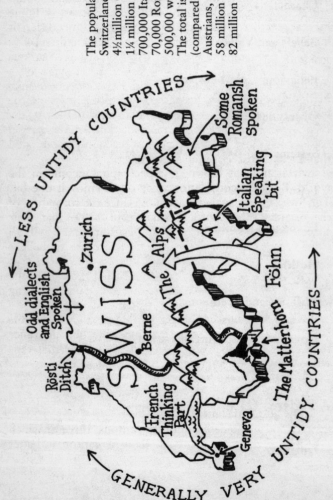

The population of Switzerland is made up of 4½ million German-speakers, 1¼ million French-speakers, 700,000 Italian-speakers, 70,000 Romansh-speakers and 500,000 who say very little. The total is just over 7 million (compared with 8 million Austrians, 57 million Italians 58 million French, and 82 million Germans).

LESS UNTIDY COUNTRIES

Some Romansh Spoken

Italian Speaking bit

Odd dialects and English Spoken

Zurich

The Alps

Berne

Rösti Ditch

French Thinking Part

Geneva

The Matterhorn

Föhn

GENERALLY VERY UNTIDY COUNTRIES

SWISS

# Nationalism and Identity

## The Physics of Fear

The laws of physics decree that the bumble bee cannot fly. Similarly, by the laws of economics, Switzerland should not be doing so sickeningly well. Land-locked, a home market smaller than London, speaking four different languages, no natural resources – other than hydroelectric power, a little salt and even less fish – no secured markets for its products through colonies or being part of a trading block, Switzerland should have come to earth with a bump long ago. Instead of which, the Swiss are the only nation to make the Germans appear inefficient, the French undiplomatic and Texans poor. The Swiss franc is a better bet than gold and the Swiss economy more solid than the granite face of the Matterhorn.

Switzerland has the highest per capita income in the world. But take consolation, they don't enjoy it one bit. The Swiss claim, as they have done since the formation of the original three-cantonal alliance in 1291, that their success is only a temporary state of affairs and it will all shortly end in tears. They stubbornly refuse to believe they are doing well and will even dispute the figures that prove it. So, like the poor donkey chasing the carrot, the Swiss pull their collective cart along ever faster, chasing the goal they passed years ago.

Perhaps it is blissful ignorance that keeps the bumble bee airborne. For the Swiss it is anything but ignorance that keeps them flying so high – it is the fear that they will one day lose everything they have worked for.

## A Federal Case

Switzerland is a federation of 26 cantons, three of which are divided into half cantons. (Half a canton is better than none.) These cantons are like miniature countries: self-financing, raising their own taxes and spending them as they want – from their own courts and police forces to education and even driving tests. Historically some were once sovereign states and many still believe they are.

The cantons comprise over 3,000 totally independent communities, each making its own decisions about such things as their welfare systems, gas, electricity, water, local roads and even public holidays.

Who controls this recipe for disaster? On the one side the federal government, and on the other the Swiss public with their unique and powerful direct voting system. By being balloted on every conceivable issue every three months, the Swiss dog actually appears to wag its own tail.

Only after digesting the diverse and independent nature of the Swiss federal system and the differences in language, culture and tradition of the country can one begin to understand the often bandied expression 'the Swiss don't really exist'. However, here they are, hidden in the centre of western Europe, in a land which bears an assortment of names – Schweiz, Suisse, Svizzera or even Switzerland. The folk who live here try very hard to persuade you that they are not 'the Swiss', but rather Zurcher, Berner, Vaudois, Luganesi, Genevois – the list is as long as the number of valleys. They have in common a red Swiss passport and a common determination not to be like the inhabitants of the next valley. In their determination to be different, the Swiss are remarkably alike.

## Three's Company

*Röstigraben* (which loses something when translated as 'fried potato ditch') is the expression coined by the Swiss media for the imaginary north-south divide between the

French-speakers, and the German-speakers. *Rösti* (pronounced rersh-tee) is the potato dish beloved of the Bernese and seen by the rest of Switzerland as symbolic of the slow, solid, dependable but starchy Swiss-German mentality. In their turn, the French-speakers refer to the '*Outre-Sarine*', those over the River Sarine or Saane, the river that flows down the fried potato ditch, implying that those who live over the river in German-speaking parts are beyond the pale.

The other divide that runs east to west between the Italian speakers and German speakers is called the Alps.

The three-way pull between the Teutonic, Gallic and Latin has all the potential discord of Belgian or Canadian divisions, not to say those of Northern Ireland or even Yugoslavia. Occasional cracks have shown in the Swiss armour like the independent-minded separatists of the French-speaking part of Canton Berne, who voted themselves a new canton, Jura, in 1978, but not before they had thrown a bomb or two.

Differences are apparent in the quarterly Swiss ballot. The German-speakers vote for the status quo and are strongly for environmental protection. The rest of the country, together with German-speaking Basle (which has only been Swiss for 500 years), vote more radically. The secret of Swiss unity is that the population has few gripes and a ready solution for any complaints with their voting system. More realistically, not to say cynically, any Swiss frictions are quickly oiled away by the best lubricant known to mankind: money.

## How They See Themselves

The Swiss have a healthy belief that whatever originates in their own country, and preferably their own area, is the best, particularly the people. Thus, if the supermarket offers Italian strawberries at half-price, the Swiss will still buy locally grown ones in the firm belief that theirs are vastly superior.

They will rarely have a good word to say about their fellow countrymen. Town-dwellers scorn their country cousins as prehistoric and naïve folk, while they in turn treat town-dwellers with deep suspicion for being too flash and smooth for their own good.

There is also intense rivalry between Swiss towns. With its international airport, high-tech industry and smoothly efficient financial sector, Zurich regards itself as the only world-class Swiss city. But, as the inhabitants of Berne are more than pleased to point out, Zurich is not the capital. The Berners find the Zurchers too much like the hard-nosed bankers of that city.

Both the slow Berners and the slick Zurchers look down on Baslers. Perilously close to France and Germany and home of Switzerland's smellier industries, Basle is thought of as being contaminated by these influences and therefore not quite Swiss-German. Baslers get their own back with their sparkling humour and will take every opportunity to pull the collective legs of their fellow cities. Hundreds of Baslers and Zurchers, both firmly convinced that they live in the best place, commute daily to each other's cities rather than move house.

Geneva, like Basle, has a reputation of being 'not quite Swiss'. Every day thousands of French pour across the border into the city to work, and a fifth of Geneva's residents has English as its first language. Clearly Geneva loses out to smaller Lausanne in the Swiss-ness stakes.

Similar rivalries are played out between the Ticino towns of Lugano and Locarno – easily confused by tourists but worlds apart to the Ticinese. But both have a brake on their antagonism by having to bow to Bellinzona, which, though smaller, is their cantonal capital.

# How They See Others

The Swiss, if happy with their strawberries, are always plagued by doubts about most other things. The biggest of these is that someone else might have thought up a better way of doing things. This leads them to look longingly over into the next valley and from there at every other nation on earth.

Switzerland is not a member of the United Nations or NATO. Officially, this is because it would compromise Swiss neutrality. Unofficially, the Swiss feel that they are not worthy to join such august organisations. They voted 'No' to joining the European Economic Area because they saw this as the start of the slippery slope to full integration with the EU. Nobody was able to convince them that there would be any great advantages in joining a poor man's club. But they have been racked with worry ever since, wondering if they made the wrong decision.

They have a long-standing love affair with America. This is because the USA is everything that Switzerland is not. America is vast and uniform. Switzerland is small and diverse. The Swiss imagine Americans to be freewheeling extrovert cowboys roaming unhindered over immense tracts of unspoilt land, while they themselves labour under a strict bureaucratic system and social codes that place heavy burdens of responsibility on every citizen's shoulders. The wildest thing that a Swiss can do is buy an American car and it is surprising how many do.

The British are admired for conquering half the world and not feeling guilty about it; and then losing it all again and not feeling a failure. The Swiss still see them as tea-sipping gentlemen despite the hordes of British football hooligans rampaging through the stadia of Europe.

The Germans are openly disliked for being so confident, not to mention being able to speak German so well. At the same time, the Swiss are secretly jealous of German confidence. The French take the collective Swiss breath away with their charm, sophistication and *savoir vivre*. And the Austrians are convenient neighbours who take the butt of many jokes.

While the Swiss adore everything from other countries in small doses, it should be noted that there is a big difference between 'things from other countries' and 'foreign'. The Swiss have trouble in defining what is Swiss, so it is clear that they will also have problems defining what is foreign. Nearly 20% of the resident population of Switzerland is foreign. You need Swiss parents, or a Swiss partner, or to be an artist, better still a rich artist, or have lived at least ten years in the country before you can be considered for citizenship.

This non-Swiss fifth of the population has provided the other four-fifths with the perfect alibi for everything that is the slightest bit imperfect. When service is poor in a restaurant, gardens are untidy, neighbours are noisy, cars are dirty, clothes not quite the latest fashion, the favourite scapegoat is saddled with the blame. With knowing looks, the explanation is proffered that the offending parties are not Swiss; they are not even tourists who are allowed to do whatever they want, but *Ausländer* – foreigners.

## How Others See Them

They tend not to. If the bumble bee's gravity-defying act represents the prowess of the Swiss economy, then the chameleon's ability to change and blend into its surroundings illustrates how the Swiss are not seen by others.

The French-speaking Swiss are hard to differentiate from unusually pernickety French. The Italian-speaking Swiss are easily mistaken for starched Italians. And the German-speaking Swiss can often be overlooked as being sedated Germans.

The culture of the Swiss is diverse, so they do not have a ready caricature. Tourists demand cuckoo clocks to take home, so the Swiss are happy to accept Swiss francs for them, but in reality they are far too kitsch for Swiss tastes and originate in southern Germany. It is true that the Swiss army is issued with knives; but not the tourist version complete with scissors, tweezers, toothpick, nail-file, corkscrew and horse-hoof stone extractor.

The Swiss are very image-conscious and care passionately how they are seen by other nations. They firmly believe that they are subject to constant inspection and criticism by the rest of the world. They do it to themselves, so they reason, others must be doing it to them too. Thus they are devastated when Switzerland is confused with southern Germany and Austria, or Sweden as it often is on the grounds that both are neutral, begin with 'Sw' and have snow. Even Switzerland's capital city is a 'Trivial Pursuits' question. It is not Geneva, nor its biggest city Zurich, nor even, as more than one tourist has thought, Interlaken, but Berne.

Such misconceptions are not helped by the liberal use of the word 'Helvetia', which has caused untold confusion among young would-be stamp collectors. Swiss cars bear the nationality plate CH. This stands for 'Confoederatio Helvetica', which means 'Swiss Federation' in Latin – the Swiss could not agree to it being in any of their own languages.

The perceptions of the Swiss as being dull and boring, while at the same time displaying a talent for ruthless efficiency and a limitless capacity for hard work, are uncomfortably close to the truth. The clichéd impressions of high mountains, watches, cheese (with and without holes), chocolate bars and gold bars are genuine.

But ask anyone in Zurich where the gnomes are and you will earn blank looks. The same applies if you want to buy a Swiss roll – no Swiss has heard of it.

# Character

With no heavy industry and no large cities, Switzerland is essentially a farming country.

Eking out any kind of existence from farming vertical slopes requires a special kind of character, not to mention farm subsidies that make the European Union's Common Agricultural Policy look like Scrooge. It's a lonely life on a mountain farm where relationships with others are more difficult to cultivate than potatoes.

Swiss farmers are tough, independent, hard-working, resilient, well-prepared for every kind of natural disaster and above all staunchly conservative. These characteristics are shared by Swiss town-dwellers, who go about their daily lives as if they too were farming a lonely mountain cliff.

The educational system does not encourage individualism. Add to this the natural introversion of an essentially mountain people and you can see why the Swiss remain deeply suspicious of those who display great self-confidence and who are articulate in public.

The terrain of their land exerts a big influence – mountains dominate the landscape and the Swiss mind-set. Thinking tends to be isolated and valley-like – always worrying what is over in the next valley and whether the grass there is greener.

## The Feel-Bad Factor

Farmers are the world's greatest complainers. Nothing is ever right for them. When it is not too dry for their crops, then it is too wet for them. The prices they obtain for their produce are never high enough.

The non-farming sector of Switzerland was quick to latch on to these qualities and so produced a nation that is never satisfied with its lot and is in constant pursuit of unobtainable improvement.

The Swiss have perfected the negative mental attitude so that it works positively. They have the happy knack of seeing the downside of any situation. Not for them the happy-go-lucky attitude that says 'It'll all come out in the wash'. They would much rather avoid getting dirty in the first place.

Müller's Law, the Swiss version of Murphy's Law, states 'Whatever can go wrong, will go wrong – but we will be more than prepared for it'.


## Don't be Happy, Just Worry

The Swiss feel that there are too many people in this world who, instead of working hard and preparing for the next disaster, are having a good time. So they have taken on their shoulders the burden of being sensible for less responsible nations – i.e., the rest of the world.

The diversity of the Swiss is apparent in the degree to which they worry. The German-speakers do little else. The French-speaking Swiss are great visionaries and philosophers with noble thoughts and global dreams. They worry that their Swiss-German compatriots do not share these dreams. The Italian-speaking Swiss have a terrible tendency not to worry nearly enough. Fortunately they account for only 10% of the population.

Living in a self-governing community with continual demands to make life and death decisions about your country's future means there is no place for frivolity. One is supposed to worry continuously and prepare for all sorts of disasters that may overwhelm the world at any time. Thus, no building may be constructed without a nuclear shelter in the cellar. The rest of post cold-war Europe relaxes, while the Swiss, in theory at least, are stocked up with provisions to survive a nuclear winter. Once a year citizens are treated to a testing of deafening alarm systems that would be used in case of flood, nuclear attack, earthquakes, volcanic eruptions, etc.

Only a Swiss government would concern itself about a small matter like running up a deficit. Only a Swiss government would devise a plan to counter the national debt problem by raising taxes. Then only the Swiss people would vote to actually pay more tax to eliminate their budget deficit.

The Swiss are the first to acknowledge that they are too serious and too preoccupied with rules and regulations. But, when it comes to the crunch, they cannot help themselves and, falling impotently under their own spell, they carry on worrying.


# Beliefs and Values

As the Swiss don't believe in themselves, they have to believe in other things instead. High on the list comes work, paperwork, education, training, God, work and the Swiss franc.


## Yodelling All the Way to the Bank

Small farmers are a classless breed and so too is Swiss society, the only real division being between the rich and the very rich. There are poor people in Switzerland, but as being poor is generally regarded as their own fault for not working hard enough, the poor keep quiet about it.

The Swiss themselves say about money: "You don't talk about it, you just have it." There is even a law supporting this: Swiss employment contracts prohibit workers disclosing their salaries to colleagues. Job advertisements are similarly prevented from stating the salary on offer.

When Mercedes introduced cars without the badges which indicate which model is which, it might have been specially for the Swiss market. It is a kind of reverse one-upmanship to buy a fantastically expensive car and then refuse to let one's neighbours know which model it is and thus how much it cost. This is how the Swiss are with their wealth. They display it, but without badges.

Not only are 500 and 1,000 franc notes in circulation, they are happily taken in payment. (1,000 Swiss francs is about £400 or US$660.) It is not unknown for Swiss housewives to pay for a loaf of bread at the local supermarket checkout with a 1,000 franc note. Bells do not ring. Security guards do not suddenly appear. The note is accepted without suspicion or rigorous inspection and given no more than a cursory glance; and, equally remarkably, the change is instantly forthcoming from the till.

## The Price is Right

Visitors to Switzerland coming from countries with weak currencies (for example, the rest of the world) must be prepared for a shock.

For the Swiss themselves, theirs is not an expensive land (naturally they deny this). The Union Bank of Switzerland annually publishes its 'Prices and Earnings Around the Globe'. This shows that, after social deductions and taxation, a Zurich bus driver earns nearly twice as much as a departmental manager from an average manufacturing company in London. And a Zurich departmental manager earns over three times more than a New York bus driver. While a New York bus driver earns nearly half that of his Zurich counterpart, the poor

London bus driver has to make do with little more than a quarter. Swiss prices are high; they have to be to pay the highest average hourly wages in the world – a worker in a Swiss supermarket can earn 20 francs an hour for stacking shelves.

## The Bells! The Bells!

Switzerland is approximately 48% Catholic and 44% Protestant. The remainder includes off-beat and occasionally suicidal sects. The church holds greater sway in Switzerland than in many modern western societies. This is witnessed by bell-ringing which the tourists find so charming but which many prematurely deaf Swiss living within earshot find rather less appealing.

Bells start clanging at all times of the day and night – to tell the farmers it is time for lunch, to tell the farmers it is time to work again; on Saturdays to remind the faithful that tomorrow is Sunday and on Sundays to tell them 'today's the day'.

Sundays, like the other six days of the week, are taken very seriously. Having flogged themselves nearly to death working through the week, the Swiss are rewarded with a genuine day of rest on Sunday. Hanging out washing, digging the garden, cleaning the car are all forbidden on Sundays. Commercial vehicles are banned and, on sunny Sundays, private motorists have a chance to see how long a queue they can make on the normally quiet Swiss roads.

The Swiss Catholic and Protestant churches are mainly financed through income taxes. Tax declarations ask for one's religious persuasion and a levy of approximately 6% per Catholic and 5% per Protestant is added to tax bills. Thus everyone is happy: Swiss atheists can benefit in the here and now by avoiding church taxes, while those paying can look on it as a form of after-life insurance.

Switzerland's Protestants, and thus a large proportion of Swiss society, have been strongly influenced by reformers like Calvin and Zwingli who advocated a simple life, and extolled the virtues of family, modesty and hard work. Buying goods on credit is still frowned upon. Saving is an essential feature of Swiss life – saving time, saving the environment and, most important of all, saving money, but not just any money: saving Swiss francs. Swiss savings per head rank second only to the Japanese. Saving up before buying is the ideal way to buy, provided one does not die of boredom first.

# Behaviour and Manners

The Swiss are seen as an unbelievably polite nation. However, their formality and reserve, not to say downright shyness, can often be mistaken for good manners.

Swiss formality manifests itself in handshaking, which is taken to absurd lengths. Even schoolchildren can be seen shaking hands when they meet and part in the street. Having spent a substantial amount in a shop, customers are bidden farewell with vigorous handshakes and from then on qualify for that establishment's handshaking list and have their hand thoroughly shaken every time they appear on the premises. All customers, regular or not, are greeted warmly in Swiss shops, and farewells include the equivalents of 'have a nice day' and Saturday's favourite, 'have a nice Sunday'.

The assorted Swiss languages do not help people to relax either. They all have a formal and a familiar form of 'you' – Sie and du, vous and tu, lei and tu. Teenagers will call each other by the familiar form from first meeting, but teenagers soon grow out of their teens and the two forms of 'you' remain as solid a barrier to close contact as any wall. One cannot even relax after crossing the hallowed divide between the formal and familiar form, as one has to then remember to always use the familiar form. It is just as rude to get it wrong the other way.

## Name Dropping

It is essential to remember other people's names in Switzerland. The Swiss are unable simply to say 'Good Morning' to their neighbours, but must always include their neighbours' name. If they cannot recall their neighbours' name, then they must remain indoors until they can.

Names are also used on the telephone. It is considered impolite to answer the telephone with 'Hello'. Swiss telephones are always answered with the surname and the caller must remember not just to say 'Goodbye', but to use the other party's name as well.

Similarly when calling, in business or privately, the Swiss always announce themselves with their surname. Thus when telephoning the station to find out the time of a train, or directory enquiries, the first thing one does is say one's name. The point of this exercise is simply to see if the other party can remember the caller's name at the end of the conversation.

## Mind Your Manners

Scrape away this formality and the classless Swiss society with farming background is revealed – with a tendency to foster manners to match. Do not expect the Swiss to queue for anything. The concept is unknown, as anyone who has witnessed the scrum for a ski-lift will attest.

In large towns pedestrians can be seen shoulder-charging each other in the streets and letting doors swing in the faces of people behind. When a bus arrives at a stop, it is devil take the hindmost, and passengers getting off have to fight their way through a seething wall of humanity all desperate to board. Escalators are witness to a similar phenomenon. Swiss town-dwellers spend most of their time rushing here and there. But the moment they set foot on an escalator they enjoy a few moments' rest. Instead of walking or standing to one side, they form an impassable stationary human snake on escalators, forcing all others to rest with them.

Coughing loudly, spitting and the amazing technique of trumpeting when nose blowing can all be witnessed in public places. Spitting is the most disagreeable, the more so in winter, when sub-zero temperatures ensure that the results remain in a deadly state of slippery suspended animation until the spring thaw.

Table manners too tend to be on the robust side, with the notable exception of wine drinking. No Swiss dare take a sip of wine in company until suitable salutations have been made to everyone at the table. These formalities can only be instituted by the host. On occasions most of a meal may have passed before the host remembers to raise his glass in the liberating toast allowing the guests to drink. At this point all conversation abruptly ceases and guests seize their glasses and hold them up high. Each diner in turn will venerate the others with a look directly in the eye and the Swiss equivalent of 'cheers' and, once again, the name of the other person. Simultaneously the glasses are chinked together to see if their host has provided real crystal. The more guests round the table, the longer this process takes – a table of four will subject the glassware to six impacts. A table of six means 15, and a table of 15 means only the most sturdy glasses, not to say wine drinkers, will survive.

The Swiss are particularly troubled by food between their teeth after meals. It certainly cannot be Swiss dentistry that is at fault. Neither is the roughage in the Swiss diet to blame. It is simply the obsessive desire to clear all traces of debris that might cause decay. Toothpicks are put to some very serious work after meals. After business lunches, businessmen can be spotted in the Gents' brushing their teeth. And where neither pick nor brush are available the Swiss will clear their teeth by sucking. This is the reason for the kissing sounds that can be heard all over Switzerland for three-quarters of an hour after each meal.

It is rude to be early and unforgivable to be late, and this is generally solved by being rudely premature rather than a few unpardonable minutes overdue.

When it comes to leaving, farewells can be on the lengthy side with neither party wishing to appear rude by wanting to leave the other. Swiss goodbyes go through a series of stages, often lasting the best part of an hour, from the initial seated declaration that it is time to go, through assorted standing phases, some without coats, some with coats on. The liveliest conversation of an evening takes place on the doorstep and out in the street.

## The Young

Traditionally children have been brought up under the Victorian-style maxim that they should be seen and not heard. Swiss education tends to be authoritarian and children have not been expected to question and challenge what they are taught. But probably as a reaction to their parents' devotion to work and the very established establishment, Swiss youth is amongst the most radical in Europe. They can afford to be radical: it is estimated that the pocket money paid out to Swiss children is roughly equal to the gross national product of some smaller African nations.

# Obsessions

## To Air is Human

The Swiss are subject to numerous obsessions. One of the strongest is their preoccupation with air.

Inside Swiss homes the uncontrolled movement of air in the form of draughts is detested. The Swiss believe that exposure for even a few seconds to a draught will bring on every ill known to mankind. Thus rigorous efforts are made during the construction of Swiss houses and apartments to eliminate the slightest possibility of a draught ever being allowed in. Yet each morning, they seem to put aside their phobia when they fling open their windows to hang the bedclothes out.

Outside their homes, concern about air quality has reached manic proportions. The Swiss even call their domestic nuclear shelters 'air protection cellars'. It is as if their landlocked island had its very own supply and it made no difference what other nations around them did with theirs.

Newspapers publish daily bulletins on the levels of ozone, sulphur dioxide and nitrogen dioxide. The level of air pollution is a political matter that rates as high in importance as the level of unemployment. Elections are won and lost on politicians' potential to deal with the air.

Switzerland was the first European country to make catalytic converters obligatory for cars and today more than three-quarters of all cars have them. All central heating boilers are regularly checked for their noxious gas content and any found to fall short of the strict limits must be replaced at the owner's expense.

The irony is that the Swiss are heavy smokers and little is done to curb this. Swiss cigarettes are amongst the cheapest in Europe and restaurants rarely have a 'no smoking' area. The Swiss quality daily newspaper *Tages Anzeiger* even refers to International No-Smoking Day as Smoking Day.

# Control and Cleanse

The Swiss have an insatiable craving to control everything and everyone in their country. All residents must
register with their local community office on moving to
an area and de-register when they move to another.

Nature too falls prey to their fixation: Swiss rivers are
no longer allowed to meander their way lazily across the
land, flooding as the fancy takes them. All Swiss rivers
run efficiently in straight lines between concrete banks
and would never dare to flood. In towns and villages
many streams are run underground in pipes to maximise
the space above ground. There is now a trend to uncover
these streams again, but they still run in manmade beds
rather than their own. High mountain pastures are
drained by elaborate sewer systems and as a result are
strewn with manhole covers.

Swiss cleanliness can go to absurd lengths. Like the
worker employed to remove chewing gum from Zurich
Airport railway station's non-slip rubber surfaced plat-
forms. Street and highways signs are not only regularly
cleaned, they are replaced with identical new signs at the
very first sign of a fleck of rust. The men of Lucerne and
Kriens even spring clean their mountain, the Pilatus, on
the third Saturday of every June by picking up the debris
and repairing the walking paths.

Having to wash the stairway to one's apartment every
so often (which is usually part of the rental contract)
seems trivial by comparison.

# No Business Like Snow Business

Swiss winters and the Swiss obsession for controlling
everything within their borders means that at times snow
has a job falling. At the sight of the first flakes, legions of

ploughs are dispatched to shove, blow and generally move the snow about the country. Farmers fit ploughs to their tractors, municipal workers leap aboard sophisticated snow handling machines, and an armada of specialised vehicles is unleashed onto autobahn, country lane and footpath to repel the white invader.

City streets, pavements, bus and tram stops are vigorously cleared of snow and ice. Large lorries take the offending material away never to be seen again. Before dawn the morning after a snowfall, householders can be seen clearing paths to their doors. Trains still run on time, planes fly in and out of airports and workers make it to factory benches and office desks with no delay in conditions that would shut down the likes of London, Paris or New York for days.

## Gone with the Wind

The wind is something that the Swiss have not yet been able to control, and in particular the great Alpine creation called the *Föhn* (pronounced somewhere between 'fern' and 'phone'). This is a wind which comes over the Alps from the Mediterranean. *Föhn* is also the German for hair drier and aptly describes what the wind is like. It blows warm air, can be very short-lived, and switches on and off, just like its namesake.

One might be mistaken for thinking that the *Föhn* is just what northern Switzerland could do with, on cold dull winter days. But no, this wind is cursed, and when it blows on come the headaches, the suicide rate goes up, car drivers start having accidents and the usually docile Swiss begin to go crazy. Other nations may blame their government and politicians for all their ills, the Swiss blame the *Föhn*.

# Environmental Wealth

Having achieved the highest living standards in the world, the Swiss turned their collective attention to the environment as long ago as the 1970s.

About half a million of the country's largest conurbation lives around the Lake of Zurich. Like all the still waters of Switzerland's lakes, this is a potential open sewer. Instead, the lake water is clear, an important drinking water supply and in summer a pleasure to swim in.

Everything that can be recycled is – glass, aluminium, steel cans, newspapers, even toilet paper. One cannot simply tip cooking fat down the drain; all such potential pollutants are deposited at special collection points to be properly treated and disposed of.

To make manufacturers use less cardboard and paper, customers are encouraged to leave packing materials behind in the shops. Milk is available in cold, clammy, floppy, one litre plastic bags to save the trees required for cartons and use less space in the rubbish bin. Paper and plastic carrier bags are, of course, re-used many times.

The Swiss public is forced to think twice about what they dispose of. In many areas rubbish is only collected when left out in officially approved refuse bags, or bags with official stickers on them. Rubbish bags and stickers cost many times more than standard bags, which has led to the phenomenon of 'rubbish tourism', whereby residents from one area take their rubbish to another community where these regulations do not yet apply. This explains why litter bins in public places are labelled 'not for household rubbish' and why they often have a padlocked cover with a small hole to allow only the smallest piece of litter to be deposited.

The Swiss have invested heavily in communal incinerators that not only burn domestic rubbish cleanly thanks to sophisticated filter systems, but also supply hot water through heavily insulated pipes for centrally heating blocks of flats. The only major drawback to this environmentalist's dream is that the Swiss have been unable to produce enough rubbish themselves to burn in the incinerators and have had to import rubbish by the truck load from Germany and Italy, at great expense, not to say environmental damage.

All new refrigerators and deep freezers can only be sold together with a coupon which the customer has to buy. This coupon is redeemable against the safe disposal of the old appliance with its ozone-layer-eating chemicals at appointed depots.

The ultimate example of recycling is that of graves. Switzerland is small and land is limited and expensive, so after 25 years under the ground, the average Swiss corpse can expect to be dug in for compost and the valuable grave re-used by someone who is in more urgent need.

## Driven up the Wall

The Swiss have a love-hate relationship with the car. On the one hand they have more Ferraris per head than any other country in the world, while on the other many Swiss are fiercely against the car.

Cars and their drivers have taken a hammering in recent years. Towns have cut the number of parking spaces, traffic lights are set to allow only half a dozen vehicles through at a time – and waiting motorists are ordered to turn off their engines as they wait or face a fine. Residents are charged hundreds of francs a year simply to park in the street without so much as a guaranteed space. Strictly enforced speed limits have been reduced and fuel prices increased by 20%. Even the country's autobahn network has been left incomplete because the anti-car lobby argues that more roads will mean more traffic. As a reaction, a political party for the down-trodden lot of the car was formed with the highly original name of the Car Party (*Auto-Partei*, now renamed the Freedom Party). It is unclear how cars are supposed to vote, but the party touched a nerve and gained seven seats in the Swiss parliament.

## Happy Birthdate

In most societies one's date of birth is sacrosanct. In Switzerland your date of birth is required for everything. You stand no hope of winning a Swiss competition unless the judges know your date of birth. From filling in the tax form to registering at a hotel, you are required to divulge your birthdate several times a day.

## Flying the Flag

There are few nations who so readily and frequently fly their flag as the Swiss. After crossing the border, one is left in no doubt that one has actually entered Switzerland – flags can be seen fluttering all over the place. Their flag is in many ways like the nation and the Helvetic typeface they gave the world – simple but distinctive. The white cross on a red background is clean, crisp and clear and it is a national flag like no other in the world – it is square, reflecting its people.

From factory to allotment, hotel to holiday home, no excuse is needed to run up the Swiss cross. Indeed, there is not only the Swiss flag to fly, each canton has its own too. Restaurant owners in the mountains run up a few flags to show potential customers toiling up towards them that their establishment is open.

# Build Quality

The Swiss long ago abandoned hope of making anything cheap and instead found a niche at the other end of the market. Of course, expensive things will only sell if they are of the highest quality and Switzerland is synonymous with quality; this has developed into yet another obsession. Swiss houses cannot make do with modern plastic gutters like the rest of the world, or even none like the USA. Swiss gutters and drain pipes are constructed from best-quality copper and, like most things the Swiss make, are built like a tank and designed to last a thousand years.

Concrete, preferably reinforced and a couple of feet thick, is one of Switzerland's favourite building materials. From churches to garden walls and mountain tunnels to autobahn flyovers, concrete is used with such alacrity one can only assume that the Swiss find it attractive.

All Swiss towns and villages are in a constant state of renovation. Cranes dominate the skyline, as building after building is refurbished. The buildings' insides are ripped out until only the shell is left. New roofs, floors, triple glazing, air conditioning, water and electricity supply, glass-fibre cabling and wall to wall luxury are installed. The end result looks uncannily like the building before the work began. It is a never-ending process. Once one building is completed workers move on to the next. After 20 years the process begins all over again.

In lesser lands a bus stop is a pole in the ground with a sign on top. Swiss bus stops are million-franc affairs which include a mains electricity supply for computerised ticket machines. The pavement in the vicinity has to be resurfaced as does the road with a special material that will not retain rainwater and thus subject waiting passengers to spray from passing vehicles. Naturally the signs require more than something as simple as the words 'Bus Stop' and each stop is labelled with its own name. After plenty of concrete has been poured, a seat is finally installed, plus a regulation litter bin for discarded tickets (but definitely not for household rubbish).

# Systems

The whole foundation and continuance of Switzerland's success is based on the development of and complete compliance with its innumerable systems. Not content with people working as hard and as efficiently as possible, the Swiss insist that all inanimate objects should also function perfectly, which they do.

No Swiss would ever consider embarking upon any enterprise, whether business or pleasure, without first having obtained the appropriate pieces of paper. These papers will then so impress all others involved, be they human or machine, that they will guarantee the successful smooth running of the operation. No Swiss car, for example, having been subject to the rigorous preparation for, and then passed the soul-searching scrutiny of, the test for vehicles over three years old would ever dare to break down.

## Public Transport

The country is criss-crossed with an elaborate mesh of trains, buses, trams, cable cars, mountain cog-wheel railways and lake steamers operated by both nationalised and private companies running together in perfect harmony. Through-tickets can be bought from one corner of the country to the other or from one mountain top to another and all services dovetail perfectly with a minimum of delay.

Public transport is more than a system and verges on being an obsession. When the new railway-timetable comes into force in May each year it is headline news, such is the interest of the Swiss public in their transport.

One hardly needs to ask if Swiss public transport is clean, efficient and punctual: 80% of trains are less than a minute late and 95% are less than five minutes late.

Money has been, and still is, heavily invested in new rolling stock, lines, tunnels and the latest technology. Add to this a few old-fashioned ingredients like hard work and you have the perfect recipe for success. A dirty Swiss train is rarer than a late one. But Swiss national railways still make a thumping loss most years.

Trains are one of the few places where the Swiss, who normally keep their emotions in check, give an outward sign of the turmoil within. Here, the calm of railway carriages is broken by the violent flicking over of newspaper pages as passengers give vent to their opinion of what they have just read in non-vocal form. Swiss railways already have special compartments where mobile phones, talking and noisy children are banned. They just need to tackle the paper flickers and they will have invented paradise on rails.

The Swiss saw no reason to abandon the tram and have continued to develop tram networks in larger towns until today their trams hardly rattle at all. Like airline pilots of the streets, learner tram-drivers take their first lessons in a multi-million franc tram-simulator before being allowed out on the rails. City trams run to a strict timetable and if a tram is a minute or so late, waiting passengers become uneasy and start to inspect the timetable at the tram stop and look at their watches. When the tram arrives the driver is given black looks and expected to explain his waywardness. Zurich tram drivers are in a constant frenzy to keep to the timetable and will actually leave passengers behind who are obviously dashing to catch the tram. In Berne, where things move much more slowly, tram drivers will annoy all the other passengers as they wait for stragglers and late-comers to board. This is the main difference between the two towns.

Thousands of items are lost every year on Switzerland's public transport system. The recovery of lost items functions smoothly under a strict system: one must be able to state the bus, tram or train line as well as the date and time when the property was lost. The trick is to lose things carefully.

## Rules of the Road

The system of driving on Swiss autobahns reflects Swiss life. There is no place for the individual to make his mark. Traffic moves in a solid mass at 5 kph (3mph) above the speed limit. (At 6 kph over the limit the cameras will swing into operation.) Travelling any slower will attract criticism from other drivers; this comes in the form of 'tailgating' – sitting so close behind the car in front as to force the driver to speed up. The only way for the Swiss driver to show any individuality is to not wear a seat belt. Only 52% of drivers wear seat belts in town, and fewer still wear them in the more individualistic French- and Italian-speaking areas. This is yet another great money spinner for the police who regularly pull in un-belted motorists and give them a hefty fine.

Being continuously fined by the police and policed by fellow drivers has made Swiss motorists an unhappy bunch. Despite tough driving tests – updated every few years incorporating two-hour written sections and exhaustive practical behind-the-wheel examinations – Swiss motorists exhibit no patience and all too often drive into one another for no apparent reason.

Their only outlet for revenge is pedestrians. Crossing

the street is a risky business even though pedestrian crossings abound. All Swiss road crossers share the common trait of walking over the road at half pace and rarely give a sideways glance at the traffic that has stopped for them. The authorities even launched a campaign to get the two parties to make eye contact – presumed better than bumper to leg contact. Little wonder that it is actually safer to cross anywhere else when one realises that 60% of all accidents between pedestrians and motorised vehicles happen on pedestrian crossings.

Swiss car number plates belong to the driver, not the car, and usually remain with the driver all his four-wheeled life. Thus the numbers reveal, not how old the car is, but how old the driver is. This system makes tracing vehicles that have been involved in a traffic offence a relatively easy task. It also provides scope for the Swiss equivalent of the nodding dog on the rear window ledge: cushions embroidered with the driver's number.

Naturally every canton has its own number plates, the first and last letters of the canton being used as a prefix, for example, GE for Geneva and BE for Berne. As a warning to other drivers, the plates of rental cars have numbers followed by a 'V' for *vermieten* – 'on hire', while the car dealers' plates contain the letter 'U' for 'untrustworthy'. And just in case inhabitants of one canton should think a vehicle from another canton is foreign, all private cars display a 'CH' nationality sticker.

# Education

In many ways Switzerland is a very old-fashioned country and things that most other societies have long abandoned all hope of, like a workable public transport system and state education, are still alive and well and flourishing. However, there are signs of changes – having waited until the late 1980s to make the start of the school year the same in all cantons, some areas have daringly experimented with dropping school on Saturday mornings.

Well-heeled parents and leading politicians still happily send their children to Swiss state schools, only resorting to the private education system if there is something wrong with their child. Examinations determine whether children will go to the equivalent of high school, secondary school or trade school.

After schooling comes training. All Swiss are trained as something, including housewives. Apprenticeships are regarded as being extremely important and whatever the job, there is an apprenticeship for it. This is no six months' on-the-job training – it is three to four years' solid studying with examinations at the end.

Teachers, who are well-paid and respected, are themselves a good example of the training system. A kindergarten teacher has a four-year apprenticeship and, in addition to school subjects, must study child psychology and three languages likely to be met in a kindergarten, like Spanish, Turkish and Serbo-Croat. A Swiss hairdresser must serve a four-year apprenticeship and a lorry driver three years. Even St Nicholas (Santa Claus), before being released on vulnerable youngsters, must attend a training course to learn what is and is not psychologically damaging to children. There is more to it than putting on a red suit, white beard and uttering "Yo-Ho-Ho".

This is why DIY has never caught on in Switzerland. It is not because the Swiss do not have enough time for it or do not need to save money by doing it themselves, it is because the Swiss do not believe it is possible to do jobs in the home oneself. It is clear that if a plumber or electrician needs four years' training, then it is work that cannot simply be attempted by untrained hands at the weekend. Even changing a light-bulb is approached with some trepidation.

The result is a highly skilled nation at every conceivable level and, until very recently, a guaranteed job for every suitably qualified candidate.

University is not the same as in other lesser lands. It is no use arriving with foreign bits of paper declaring the holder's achievements. They are worthless, and entry to the hallowed portals of a Swiss university is only possible by obtaining the appropriate Swiss qualifications. The Swiss will then tell you that their degrees are of a far higher standard and thus more worthwhile than those available elsewhere.

## Swiss Army Life

The Swiss army is not only famous for its knives, but also for the fact that every Swiss male from 20 to 40 is a member.

Far from being a land of pacifists, Switzerland is aggressively neutral with a potential army of over half a million. All these troops go about their daily jobs – banking, farming and so on – while in their wardrobes at home hang their uniforms, and, more amazing still, in the attic cupboard lie their guns and ammunition. It is not unusual to see men out of uniform on bicycles or the tram with a submachine gun slung over their shoulder. They are just on the way to keep their trigger fingers trained with a bit of compulsory shooting practice.

The Swiss have finally acknowledged the contradiction of the situation whereby they have a huge army yet have not had a decent war for over 500 years. Thus the army is being streamlined to 400,000 men and cuts are being made. For example, carrier pigeons have recently been dispensed with.

It has been argued that the reason for the dearth of wars is Switzerland's impressive defence capability. But the truth is that no power-crazed dictator is going to attack the country where he has stashed away his secret millions.

# Leisure and Pleasure

For centuries the conservative Swiss thought that mountains were only for raising cows and blowing alphorns on. Then, thanks in great part to the carefree British upper classes in the early part of the 20th century, things changed. Cows are still milked and alphorns still sound their melancholic blast, but the chocolate-box countryside now rings to some new tunes.

## To Ski or Not to Ski, That is the Question

The Swiss have never tackled skiing with the same fanaticism as visitors from low-lying countries. Good sense, national caution and the fact that there are mountains within less than an hour's reach from anywhere in Switzerland, means that skiing is approached with an air of nonchalance. Only when the weather and snow is perfect will the Swiss be found in any numbers on the pistes. It goes without saying that they all learned to ski before they could walk. Even so, they will spend as much time eating, drinking and sitting in the sun as they will on their skis.

Much more pleasing to them is the fact that other nations are potty about the sport and are willing to come and spend a fortune in Swiss ski resorts. Many ski-lifts and ski areas are owned by farmers. As a result, the ski-lifts often do not interconnect and one has to walk some distance from the end of one ski-lift to the start of the next. Farmer Müller sees no reason on earth why he should extend his lift at his expense to send customers on to farmer Meier's lift. Swiss skiers look upon these gaps in the lift system as an ideal opportunity to warm up their muscles with a stiff march.

## Walking and Talking

The robust sport of *Wandern*, hiking, or at the very least walking briskly, is eagerly pursued by the hardy Swiss-Germans in particular. Their part of the country is choked with intricate webs of paths for walking. When meeting on these paths, they greet each other with a secret code word. This word is *Grüetzi* or some variation of it. From the way this word is spoken the hearers are able to tell where the other party comes from. This will often lead to extended debate among fellow walkers that only ends when more walkers are met and *grüetzi*-ed. Whence the debate starts again with renewed vigour.

The French-speaking Swiss are not so keen on walking and in the Italian-speaking part the only people to be seen walking are *grüetzi*-ing German-speaking Swiss on holiday.

## Going on a Summer Holiday

The months of July and August see a drain of the population away from their work desks. City bus and tram timetables are cut as drivers and passengers alike go on holiday.

Many Swiss are content to holiday within their own borders. The mountain scenery is hard to better elsewhere and they know the food will be good, the plumbing efficient and leaving one's own canton is virtually going abroad anyway. Nevertheless, high wages and the strong

Swiss franc mean that the Swiss are frequent, if inconspicuous, world-travellers. Before you take out a second mortgage on a holiday-of-a-lifetime in Bali, be warned the place is full of Swiss supermarket-checkout staff – all of whom have paid for their holiday in cash.

## Workers' Playtime

Hard work is followed by hard play. A diverse and individual nation produces diverse and individual spare-time pursuits.

Swiss summers see towns and villages turning out in droves to watch *Schwingen* festivals. This is a peculiarly Swiss form of amateur wrestling in which burly young men wearing T-shirts and baggy shorts on top of their trousers wrestle each other to the ground. In the tiny Bernese hamlet of Unspunnen the normally sensible folk, tired of throwing each other to the ground, devised their own sport of wrestling a stone, called the *Unspunnenstein* – the stone of Unspunnen. Tough and foolhardy types see who can toss the rock, weighing as much as a man, the furthest. For those wanting to avoid a hernia there is another form of *Schwingen*, *Fahnenschwingen* or wrestling the flag, in which the flag usually wins.

*Hornussen* is a version of golf played with bendy clubs by men without the slightest sense of correct golf-course dress. Small black plastic yo-yos are whacked from large wedge-shaped tees. Other intrepid, not to say downright stupid, players then try to intercept these missiles by throwing large home-made bats in the air. The bats look suspiciously like 'beware of the bull' signs wrenched from some nearby field.

Switzerland has no less than 29 officially registered circuses, and there is hardly a town or village which is not host to a circus during the year.

As with the rest of Europe, the Swiss are great soccer fans. The less energetic play *Jass* (pronounced 'yas'), a card game which employs a unique set of cards and functions under rules that only those born and brought up in Switzerland can have any hope of ever understanding. *Jass* is so popular that not only is it played in every spare moment in every corner of every restaurant, but there is even a weekly television programme devoted to it.

The Swiss are also keen collectors. Such everyday items as the foil tops of coffee creamers depicting various themes are avidly sought after. Customers in restaurants can be seen licking the backs of the creamer covers then wiping them with paper napkins. It is considered very *bünzlig* (stodgy and boring) to collect these, so the creamer tops are slid into pockets with the assurance that they are being collected for a young nephew. Albums to mount creamer tops are available in stationery shops, and complete sets of limited editions have achieved thousands of francs at auction.

When the country was flooded with counterfeit 5-franc pieces the police were unable to get their hands on more than one example of the thousands of forgeries. It was soon discovered that the Swiss were eagerly collecting the coins. Before long the 5-franc forgeries were changing hands among collectors at up to 150 francs each.

## Boxing Clever

The Swiss watch much less television on average than other nations. This reflects not so much the intelligence of the Swiss as the poor quality of their programming. Every country gets the television it deserves and Switzerland is no exception. The difference is that Switzerland gets everyone else's as well.

The hilly terrain and aversion to television aerials (which

in many areas are banned from the roofs of houses) result in most Swiss homes being served by cable television. This provides an average of 50 channels in most areas.

Swiss television, which is, of course, available in German, French, Italian and at odd times in Romansh, tends to be somewhat earnest in its output. The mainstay is hours of debate over the pros and cons of forthcoming referenda, and some of the more obscure Swiss sports. Sit-coms, called Swiss-coms, are rare and even more rarely successful.

Like much of continental television, Swiss television relies heavily on announcers. These are usually women who explain at length what the next programme is all about so that those who have better things to do need not watch it.


# Eating and Drinking

Swiss food is as diverse as the land itself. Nearly every town and village has its own speciality – cake, pie, dessert, sausage, wine, etc. And if it has not, one is soon invented to sell to tourists. Food plays an important part in Swiss life. The number of restaurants bears witness to this. No mountain top is complete without one, and the difficulty with which one finds an empty restaurant seat confirms the popularity of eating out.

After their early morning start, the Swiss soon feel peck-ish and eat their elevenses at 9 o'clock. By mid-morning they cannot hold off any longer and need their lunch. Lunchtime is a big event in Switzerland and can stretch to over an hour and sometimes two even on working days. From 11 a.m. onwards the Swiss greet one another with food salutations like '*Bon appetit*' and '*En Guete*' (have a good one) to get the saliva glands going. Shops close, children come home from school and fathers will pop back from the office if it is not too far away.

Lunch is tax deductible to the tune of 2,800 francs a year even if eaten at home. Thoughtfully, nightworkers can also deduct the same amount for their meals, although their chances of finding anywhere serving food after 10 p.m. are less than slim.

The day's early start means the evening meal is often over by 6.30 p.m. But never mind, this allows the Swiss an early night so that they can get up at the crack of dawn again the next day.


## The *Muesli* Belt

*Muesli*, the invention of the Swiss, Dr Bircher-Benner, is not so much a breakfast cereal in its native land as a creamy fruit-filled stomach liner that is more often eaten at lunchtime.

Swiss meals are prepared with care and fresh vegetables, and eaten slowly with appreciation. Most Swiss housewives scorn television dinners, frozen and convenience foods. So, too, microwave ovens and even electric kettles are regarded as unnecessary. For many Swiss, fast food is simply too quick.

The German-speaking Swiss brought the world *Rösti* – potato shreds fried in butter. They also have a tendency to indulge in *Metzgete* (literally butchery) – assorted parts of pigs, from trotters to bulging blood and liver sausages.

The Swiss are not a nation of animal lovers as their restaurant menus prove, with horse steak often on offer. Most towns have a horse butcher's – it is the only shop with no windows – but despite being a little coy about displaying their wares, the popularity of horse meat continues; one Swiss paper could not have put it better when it reported 'Horse Meat Remains Stable'.

Menus vary with the seasons and autumn brings *Wild Menüs*. Not quite as exciting as it might sound, these are game dishes. Venison is accompanied by chestnuts, red cabbage and *Spätzli* (pasta-like cooked dough), all washed down with *Sauser*, young and partly fermented wine which is red, a little bubbly and good for diarrhoea – getting it, not stopping it.


# Drink

The Swiss hold their drink well and at the very worst become talkative, but even then not always. Alcohol is freely available and street vendors of hot dogs sell cold beer to go with them. Draught beer, a lager brewed by dozens of local breweries but always tasting the same over the whole country, is cheaper than mineral water.

Mineral water is a perfect example of how Switzerland functions. Most people from outside the country would be hard pressed to name a Swiss mineral water. But what about Perrier? French you think? Yes, the water is French. But the important part, the shares, are Swiss.

Swiss wines do not have an international reputation because they rarely get out of the country since the Swiss drink them all themselves. Spirits, other than *Schnaps*, are not popular and are expensive. However, when whisky or gin is doled out, it is in generous measure and usually accompanied with a very nice view.

Switzerland has its own soft drink specialities. What Dr Bircher did with *muesli* – i.e., make something healthy and at the same time palatable – the Swiss drinks company Rivella has succeeded in doing with its peculiarly Swiss soft drinks. These are made from the milk by-product whey, and are not so unpleasant as one would first suspect. Eagerly consumed by those Swiss who no longer count themselves in the Pepsi generation, Rivella is even available in a sugar-free light version.

The Swiss long ago mastered the making of coffee and serve some of the best in the world – strong, full of taste and never bitter. The same cannot be said for their tea. There is no plant, flower or weed that the Swiss have not cut, dried and then brewed into some sort of tea. There is tea for the liver, tea for the heart, tea for the bladder, tea to wake one up and tea to send one to sleep.


# Health

Switzerland has an array of very sensible and efficient health funds. These are similar to health insurance, except that they are not supposed to make money out of their customers' ill health.

The funds do not normally cover dentists' charges. If they did, the money would have dried up long ago. Such are Swiss dentists' fees that it is cheaper to fly anywhere in the world and have one's teeth treated privately than let a Swiss dentist loose in one's mouth. There is even a trade in 'Dental Holidays' to countries like Hungary where one can fly, stay in a first-class hotel, spend a week shopping in between daily dental treatment and still make a substantial saving on Swiss prices.

Despite their charges, Switzerland is rife with dentists, with one for every 1,443 mouths (which is over double the number of dentists per head compared with Britain). The figure for Swiss psychiatrists is not available.

Because of the high cost of dental treatment, the Swiss take great care of their teeth. At 250 francs a filling and 2,000 francs for a crown, their mouths very soon become a substantial investment.

# Doctors and Nurses

Switzerland boasts a very low ratio of patients to doctors, and patients to hospital beds and, happily for the doctors, a high ratio of nurses to doctors. With all this medical supervision, waiting lists for operations do not exist and Swiss life-expectancy is above average – for men 75 years and women 82.

The north-eastern canton of Appenzell operates a remarkably un-Swiss concept; it allows anyone to set up as a medical practitioner. Thus this little corner of the land is crammed full of every conceivable health cure from herbalist to faith-healer and more than their fair share of crackpots.

More conventional and traditional treatment in the form of spas and mountain convalescent homes are found all over the country. The Swiss are very interested in medical matters, the more so when eccentric millionaires are willing to pay vast sums in search of the fountain of youth or for a brain transplant.

Although as a nation they care little about the effects of smoking or their cholesterol levels, they succumb quite frequently to *Lungenentzündung* – pneumonia. When not brought low with pneumonia, the Swiss suffer with numerous circulation ailments – *Kreislaufstörungen*. These problems vary from the relatively minor *Blutstau*, a blood blockage or dam, to a complete collapse of the circulation – *Kreislaufkollaps*. Any one of these complaints might be fatal in its own right, but the Swiss suffer nearly continuously from one or sometimes all of them at once.

Luckily, sufferers rarely need even so much as a day off work. The secret is tea. Having diagnosed the problem, the patient merely selects the correct tea for the disease, drinks a couple of litres and puts him or herself to bed. Bingo – the next morning they are at work again bright and early.

Most Swiss over 25 are regularly brought low by *Hexenschuss* (lumbago), literally 'a witch's shot'. These witches generally seem to shoot their victims in the back. The remedy is a little physiotherapy paid by the health fund and, naturally, tea for the back.

Leading in every sphere, the Swiss have also achieved the highest occurrence of AIDS in western Europe. The Swiss medical profession is quick to point out that, like most of the other facets of Swiss life, it is simply that they know more about what is going on in their country.

## Hygiene

Hygiene is one of the cornerstones of Swiss life. The most desirable attribute a Swiss can display is to be *gepflegt* or *soigné* – well groomed or well cared-for. Women grade and reject potential suitors on their standards of personal hygiene.

Strangely, the Swiss allow dogs into their restaurants, yet many a modest restaurant has toilets which are not only large enough to accommodate every customer if they were all caught short at the same time, but the quality of fittings and overall cleanliness means one could literally eat one's dinner off the floor.

Not content with this, the Swiss put their minds to solving the age-old problem of lavatory seats in public places. At the press of a button, a cover glides round to grace the seat with a new section of never-before-sat-on plastic. Many homes boast a great Swiss lavatorial invention that can take one's breath away (or at least make one's eyes water). The Swiss have combined the flushing W.C. with the bidet and the warm-air dryer to produce the ultimate in lavatorial luxury – the all dancing, all electronic Closomat. This dispenses in one blow with the need to use toilet tissue or even wash your hands.

# Customs and Traditions

Switzerland is brimming with customs and traditions. Many are local and some distinctly odd, like in the northeast of the country where, to celebrate the Julian New Year (which is a few weeks after the rest of the world's New Year), the normally staid citizens can be seen wandering through the fields at night with anything from a dolls' house to a botanical garden over their heads.

## A Year in Providence

The Swiss year runs to a tight timetable. It starts with a bang at New Year, and the celebrations, which include fireworks, champagne and parties, are so intensive that in some cantons 2nd January is also a holiday.

The festive season ends on 6th January with 'Three Kings' Day'. Special cakes are sold with a small plastic king hidden in the pale dough. The lucky child who finds the king and does not choke to death on it gets to wear a paper crown the rest of the day and order around the rest of the family.

February brings enough snow even for the fussy Swiss to take to skis, and schools have two weeks' 'sport holidays'. This month also brings *Fastnacht*, the carnival period when outlandish costumes are worn with masks and painted faces. Festivities ensue with plenty of eating and drinking, and satirical songs and skits are performed. Swiss carnival-goers get up at 5 a.m. or earlier, wrap up warmly, and then proceed to wake up everyone else. During this period the Swiss can dress however ridiculously they want in public and no-one will bat an eyelid.

The Swiss work ethic is perfectly illustrated by Zurich's annual spring half-day holiday called *Sächsilüüte* (pronounced sax-ee-lootah) or six o'clock ringing. For this celebration, the town of Zurich gets a Monday afternoon off work. Having gone to work on Monday morning as usual, shortly after lunch the holiday begins. The guilds parade through the town and then gather to watch the burning of a paper snowman. This is all to celebrate the fact that winter has gone and, with longer hours of daylight, the guildsmen can work longer hours again.

The day before Good Friday is called 'Green Thursday' but treated, and therefore referred to, as a 'Saturday' for working-hour purposes, i.e., shops and offices close early. These 'Saturdays' occur throughout the year before holidays. The day before the Ascension Day holiday is one, so is Christmas Eve, unless it is a Sunday.

In May Swiss wardrobes start to change. Winter clothes are hung neatly in moth-proof cabinets in attics, and lightweight short-sleeved summer clothes are brought out. Before summer proper can begin, the 'Ice Saints' have to make their appearance with their last cold blast of winter. Only when this danger is past is one allowed to plant out geraniums in window boxes.

During the summer months there is not a town or village in the land that does not mount its own special celebration. Some are steeped in history and serve special purposes like the *Fêtes des Vendanges* of the French-speaking Swiss when processions give thanks for the harvest and in particular the wine vintage. Other festivities are nothing more than an excuse for the Swiss to do what they like best (after working) – namely, sitting for hours at long, uncomfortable, wooden trestle tables eating grilled sausages and downing plastic beakers of beer or wine.

Because Swiss summers and winters are well-defined seasons, good advantage is taken of the warmer months. The longer days see public open-air swimming baths opening round the lakes and town pools. Restaurants block the pavements with tables and chairs. The final confirmation that good weather is on the way is the start of the annual digging up and resurfacing of the autobahn network just when it is at its busiest.

When schools close for the summer holidays, much of Switzerland closes with them. Summers are surprisingly hot and thundery in low-lying towns and so, given half a chance, their inhabitants leave.

1st August is Swiss National Day, which means more fireworks and trestle tables. Considering how widely the day is celebrated it is surprising to learn that it was not until 1995 that 1st August was made a public holiday in every canton, and only then after the customary vote.

Summer usually ends in a massive thunderstorm on a Sunday evening in mid-August. The cooler days that follow let the Swiss get down to some hard work again. But local festivities continue with an unrelenting round of street parties, school-class reunions and local club parties – every hobby has a *Verein* or club, and every club has a party.

Christmas in Switzerland is a very downbeat affair. Families gather quietly round real Christmas trees with real candles and a quiet old time is had by all. The Swiss are shocked by British and American Christmases which involve heavy drinking, heavy eating and heavy television watching. Party hats and crackers have no place at a Swiss Christmas. The main focus is on the evening of December 24th. Naturally this is a normal working day, reduced to 'Saturday' status in deference to the season. The big advantage of getting all the festivities behind one on the 24th is that there are then two clear days to get ready to go back to work. If the Swiss tradition for work is seen anywhere, it is seen over the festive season. Should Christmas and New Year fall over the weekend, there are no extra weekdays off in lieu. It's back to work on Monday and better luck next year.

Throughout the year celebrations are accompanied with special food – the Three Kings' Cake on 6th January, gingerbread men without any gingerbread in them at St Nicholas (6th December). Christmas is no different, and for many housewives the advent period is spent making biscuits. Each has her own personal or favourite recipe for a dozen or more varieties. Buying them ready-made from a shop is frowned upon and, as if there was not enough to do in the pre-Christmas period, these biscuits require hours of preparation and baking at home.

One would have thought there would be nothing nicer once the baking was over than to put one's feet up and enjoy the fruits of one's labour. But no: the biscuits are not for eating oneself. They are packed into little tins and packets and handed round to friends. These friends, who have also been slaving for hours in the kitchen, will present their offerings too. The end result of this swop is that everybody ends up with biscuits which they consider much inferior to their own.

## Music of the Folk

The Swiss get very upset when the much more widespread um-pah-pah music of Germany is mistaken for theirs. Swiss folk music, known as *Hudigääggeler* (pronounced Hoodee-gackela), is a distinctive blend of accordion, clarinet and double bass usually played by a trio, except when there are four of them. Sometimes a *Hackbrett* – literally a chopping board – is also played. This is like a zither, but instead of being plucked, its strings are whacked with a couple of wooden spoons.

The fact that there are only three pieces of *Hudigääggeler* music has not prevented it being played day and night throughout the land. There is even a radio station that plays the three tunes back-to-back 24 hours a day. The Swiss like this music for the sole reason that it is not foreign.

47

Not as convenient to carry as a mouth organ, but somewhat louder, is the alphorn. (Not be confused with the *alpenhorn*, which is for storing and keeping breakfast cereals fresh.)

Like the alphorn, yodelling was originally devised as a kind of telephone system for mountain farmers. Today it is just as popular in the lowlands. There are even occasional yodelling church services. The call of the lone yodeller is a melancholic one, mainly because yodelling has spread throughout the world (there is even a yodelling club in Japan) and the Swiss have not made a penny out of it.

# Government and Bureaucracy

Switzerland is no socialist state. Its citizens rise and fall by their own doing. There is no attitude that says it is the government's fault when things go wrong or the government can pay when there is a financial problem. Through their federal system, the Swiss are too close to their government to be able to blame it, and when the government pays, they know who will have to pay the government – they will.

## Democracy Gone Mad

The Swiss federal system is like democracy gone mad. If citizens can scrape together enough signatures, they can have any issue put to the vote. Only Swiss good sense has so far prevented irresponsible proposals like 'free beer for all'.

The Swiss government is not confrontational as in the UK or USA, where the right is opposed to anything the left says, and vice versa. There is in effect no opposition to the Swiss government in the traditional sense. However, more and more the Swiss people are providing, if not an opposition, certainly a check on the government's proposals. Left to its own devices, the Swiss government would have had the country in the European Union, fielding soldiers within the United Nations, and VAT would have been in force years ago. But the people are consulted every quarter and they let the government know their thoughts on the matter through the ballot box.

The 200-seat Swiss National Council has been elected by a form of proportional representation since 1919 and is composed of no less than 13 political parties, the smallest two having one seat each. These parties cover the complete political spectrum: the Radical Democrats are counterbalanced by the Christian Democrats, the Greens and 'red' socialists are tempered by the conservative *bürgerliche* block. But whatever the political colour, the end result is all rather grey.

For those not in favour of proportional representation there is a second body called the Council of States to which each canton, regardless of size or population, sends two representatives. It has to send two, to enable half cantons to send one.

There is no head of state or prime minister, but a ceremonial position of an annually rotating presidency – after all, someone has to entertain visiting foreign dignitaries. Thus the Swiss will often be hard pressed to name their president because he or she (Switzerland has now had its first woman president) is not very important and there is a new one each year.

The whole system seems a guaranteed formula for deadlock and gridlock. But with votes of 'no-confidence' and impeachment forbidden, Switzerland has one of the most stable governments in the world. Although there is a parliamentary election every four years, dramatic political swings to the left or right appear impossible. The result is that the stock market, Swiss business and commerce are free to invest and plan without keeping a weather eye on a changing political climate. However, the responsibility for half-governing their country puts a great strain on the average Swiss: no less than 12% of the population who die before they are 72 die by their own hand.

## Vote For Me

There is a danger that the Swiss spend most of their free time voting. They vote for their National Assembly every four years. In between they have to vote for their Cantonal government, not to mention casting ballots for local town and community councillors. They are also supposed to attend and vote at their local council meetings. Add to this the demand to divulge their opinions in quarterly referenda and it is no surprise that even the most stalwart Swiss voter can succumb to 'voter fatigue' – a sort of voter's version of housemaid's knee. The reality is that on average, barely more than 40% of those entitled actually cast their votes.

Voting papers are delivered to Swiss homes a month before a ballot. This is with good reason as it would take all day to fill in the papers at the polling stations. Advice pours in from all quarters – newspaper advertisements, posters and direct mail – imploring a 'yes' or a 'no' vote on referendum matters.

When it comes to electing members to parliament, things reach epic proportions. There are dozens of political parties to choose from. These range from the conventional to the 'Thank Goodness We've Got Beat Looser Party'. Beat Looser is a young man who goes to the same tailor as their famous folk-hero, William Tell. There is a green party for the over-60s, known as the 'Greys'; the 'Men's Lib Party'; and the sinister-sounding 'National

Action Party Against Over-foreigning'. (But if they got rid of their foreigners who could they blame?)

Recommended lists are printed which contain ideal political groups enabling voters to make a table d'hôte selection. Alternatively, voters can go à la carte and make up their own lists from personal favourites. Just to confuse matters, these do not even have to be names taken from the lists – anyone Swiss and over 18 can be added, and voted for. It all sounds rather exciting and in theory it could be. In reality it is not.

Despite such a bend-over-backwards democracy, like the rest of the world the Swiss have a healthy disregard for those they elect to power and criticise their elected representatives' every move.


## Your Papers Please

The Swiss make other countries' bureaucracies look like amateurish cottage industries. Before anything can be done in Switzerland, a piece of paper giving permission for the activity must first be obtained.

The governmental decision-making process is never rushed. The Swiss try to understand all the whys and wherefores of a situation before coming to a conclusion. This saves wasting time if anything goes wrong. It also means that it can take a very long time to come to any sort of a decision. Long-term planning and solutions rather than short-sighted goals are the order of the day, or should it be year? Whatever the Swiss decide on, it is meant to last a long time; if possible, forever.

The authorities want to know where you are and all about you all the time. In addition to de-registering at your local community office when moving, and re-registering with your new community within eight days, every Swiss family has a 'family book' issued by their home town. This is a substantial hard-backed book like an oversized passport giving details of the family members, presumably in case one ever forgets.

In order to launch a boat with more than 15 square metres of sail on a Swiss lake, the craft must be registered. Would-be drivers of motorboats have to past a test and obtain a licence before being allowed behind the wheel. If the boat is powered, the engine must be inspected to ensure the emissions do not exceed strict limits. Bicycles need an annually renewable sticker to show they are insured. Cars must display a sticker to drive on the auto-bahns, another to park in the streets at night and yet another to show the vehicle has passed the stringent exhaust emissions test.

This bureaucratic stranglehold would appear to be highly inefficient, but this is Switzerland. Every time a piece of paper is issued, amended, updated or withdrawn, it costs money. The state does not pay; the owner of the piece of paper forks out, handsomely. Thus in a stroke the Swiss have converted a potentially top-heavy bureau-cracy swimming with civil servants into a self-financing and highly efficient industry that makes capitalism and privatisation look like child's play.

# Business

Add together pharmaceuticals, chocolates, cheese, watches, precision instruments and specialised heavy machinery. Throw in banking, financial services and insurance, and finally for good measure tourism, and you have the economy with a higher gross national product (GNP) per capita than any other country on earth, without the trade surplus or economic problems of Japan.

Swiss business has experienced 40 years of almost unbroken boom. For most of this period the Swiss were unaware that 'zero unemployment' as understood by Keynsian economics means around 2% of the working population. During the mid 1990s unemployment in Switzerland reached unheard-of levels: in excess of 5%. It is now tumbling in the direction of the pre '90s when the Swiss ran their unemployment rate at 0.4% – or less than 18,000 people. They probably knew them all by name.

## Stress the Stress

Stress is an important ingredient in the Swiss formula for business success. Ask working Swiss how their job is and you will be regaled with morbid tales of how stressful their occupation is. They will emphasise how there are simply not enough hours in the day to fulfil their duties to perfection.

Ask the British and you will be given a typical under-stated summary of how they are 'not too busy' and how things 'aren't too bad'. Such cool, laid-back responses would be interpreted by the Swiss as the utterings of the work-shy and a blatant admission of the worst of all crimes, laziness.

Unemployment benefit, though generously paying up to 80% of one's previous salary, stops after 18 months. This, and the fact that there is no statutory redundancy payment, keeps the Swiss on their toes. As a result they spend unreasonably long hours at their places of work looking worried and generally complaining about the volume of work they have to do.

The standard working week is 42 hours and all Swiss will tell you that they personally work far longer than this. Why have they not voted themselves a shorter working week? It was proposed, but they voted against it.

# Time is Everything

'Time is Everything' was the advertising slogan of the national airline, Swissair, and it could easily be the maxim for all Swiss business too. The Swiss are so punctual that they have a concept incomprehensible to lesser nations, that of being Überpünktlich – literally, over punctual – and it is not viewed as a fault. Significantly, when Swiss-Germans want to know the time they do not ask "What's the time?", but "How late is it?"

Swiss business sticks to traditional ideas where these have proved successful, like paying women less for doing the same job as men and having the meanest maternity leave in Europe, while at the same time jumping at the latest technological developments. Swiss business was amongst the first in the world to make use of computers. Today a Swiss businessman would rather be seen without his trousers than without his mobile phone.

At the higher echelons of management, dress conventions are quite strict, but at middle and lower management levels, the Swiss are surprisingly casual dressers at work. Office staff, both male and female, will often be dressed in jeans.

Paper qualifications hold great sway. Job applicants who 'seem just right for the job' can forget it if they do not have the correct pieces of paper. These will include references from previous employers which are couched in special coded language. Thus 'Mr X worked to our satisfaction' is a poor reference, whereas 'Mr X worked to our complete satisfaction' is an excellent one.

# Low Taxes

Swiss commerce and industry, as well as the people, thrive under what is essentially an old-fashioned but very workable tax system. Income tax is collected locally, where one lives. Thus two individuals working side by side in the same business receiving the same salary can pay different amounts of tax if they live in different communities.

Capital gains tax does not exist in many cantons, death duties are minimal between generations, and value added tax, introduced as late as 1995, is a derisory 7.5%. There is a wealth tax, but even with a million in the bank it is less than 1% a year. A whole host of items are tax deductible, from mortgages on as many homes as one can afford, without any limit on the amount, to what the Swiss regard as a business necessity, bribes.

Income tax is paid retrospectively and bills are sent out to be paid in three instalments or one lump (with a discount for prompt payment). To minimise the shock of the tax demand, Swiss employers pay a thirteenth month's salary at the end of each year to pay the tax bill. This would put taxes at one twelfth, or 8.3%, which is optimistic even by Swiss standards. The Swiss pay on average only about 16% tax and still grumble about it.

After death the authorities are quickly on the scene to establish that the departed has paid all taxes due. You can't take it with you, but the Swiss authorities suspect its citizens might try.

## What About the Workers?

The Swiss work force is highly trained, highly skilled and highly paid. A no-strike pact was agreed in the late 1930s and industrial stoppages are virtually unknown. In reality the Swiss have a job to think of anything to strike about.

All this training, harmony and high pay created one problem: who was going to dig holes in Swiss roads? The answer came in the form of the seasonal workers or *saisonniers*. Mainly from Mediterranean countries, these seasonal 'guest workers' send their hard-earned Swiss francs to their families back home each month. When the job is finished, the Swiss authorities in turn send the workers back home to their families – neatly exporting Swiss unemployment.

A remarkable 124,000 workers, 4% of the Swiss work-force, come to Switzerland just for the day – 47,000 from Germany, 5,000 from Austria, 32,000 from Italy and 40,000 from France. These day-trippers are wooed over the border to earn, on average, double the money they would get in their own country for doing the same job.

Swiss tradesmen are called in at great expense to perform the smallest of tasks in the home (other than cleaning). Highly trained they may be, but clearly the first thing they learn on the first day of their four-year training course is to declare whatever job they were called in to perform, 'impossible'. Before tackling any project, how-ever straightforward, they will, with a theatrical intake of air between the teeth, state categorically that what they have been asked to do simply cannot be done. Swiss householders then have to spend at least half an hour per-suading them that it is possible.

Finally the worker agrees, does a wonderful job and adds the half hour persuasion time to his bill.


# Who Sells What to Whom and Where

The nation's shops reflect the Swiss desire to hang on to what they like as long as it works. Retail distribution is still relatively old-fashioned and depends heavily on the importer, wholesaler and small shop. Shop opening hours are strictly regulated and Sunday opening is forbidden, except, of course, where tourists want to spend their Swiss francs.

The Swiss do not shop around for the lowest price – they do not have the time and, while they may not need to save money, they will never waste it. Part of Switzerland's success is due to its consumers' preference for Swiss products. The foreign alternatives may be cheaper, but the Swiss buy Swiss because they believe their goods will work better and last longer – and they are usually right.

Swiss consumers have been helped in their support of the small shops by a strong retail lobby. Chemists make sure that supermarkets cannot sell aspirins, and retailers of domestic appliances object vigorously to any plans to build 'superstores' in their area. The result is that the small specialist retailer is still in business, if only just. Out-of-town shopping centres exist, but they have yet to make the same massive inroads into the conventional retail trade as elsewhere.

Cartels, long declared illegal in most western economies, still thrive in Switzerland. From time to time the government takes a shot at them and cartels have to defend their position. In many trades and industries the key players get together and decide on such un-free market tactics as where their products will be sold and at what price.

As long ago as 1925 it was seen that there was scope to bring down Swiss retail price levels when a certain Gottlieb Duttweiler started a direct sales operation. With only six products, he undercut established retailers' prices by up to 40%. Duttweiler split gross packets of basic foodstuffs like coffee, rice, pasta and sugar into demi-grosses and the Swiss institution Migros was born. Today, other than a small pocket of the country which includes St Moritz, there is not a community in the land that is not served by one of its 560 stores.

Logic should dictate that after more than three-quarters of a century Migros should have closed down all its competitors. It has not, and despite having a finger in numerous pies from banking to service stations, Migros has never been able to shed its down-market image in the way, for example, Marks & Spencer has in Britain. Buying food at Migros is regarded as being sensible. But no Swiss would dream of buying presents there – that would be looked upon as being one step beyond thrifty: plain mean.

# Crime and Punishment

Switzerland is often referred to as a police state, particularly by fans of microlite aircraft, snowmobiles and jet skis, all of which are banned within its borders.

One explanation for this is the misuse of the word translated into English as 'police'. There are the 'dead pets police' for disposing of dead pets. There are the 'lake police' on the lakes (a very pleasant job in summer). To oversee the eligibility of foreigners to work and reside in the country there are the 'foreign police' (who are not foreign at all). Checking on the correct disposal of household rubbish are the 'rubbish police'. One of the most horrendous crimes that one can commit is to put out one's rubbish in a non-approved bag. The rubbish police will sift through the contents of offending bags for clues to the culprit and fines can be quite steep, even for the first offence.

Switzerland is thick with laws and even thicker with their enforcement. This very occasionally falls flat on its face, like when it was found that there was no law to prevent a Zurich businessman from painting his own parking space outside his office. There are times when the dogged appliance of rules seems to rule out common sense. Cinema goers are treated to an intermission, however short the movie. The projectionist pulls the plug at the designated moment, regardless of the action on screen at the time. Taking a bath before 7 a.m. or after 10 p.m.

is forbidden in most apartment dwellers' book of rules. But since it is unthinkable that any Swiss would arrive at their office desk at dawn (as most do) without washing, showers are exempt from such rules.

The Swiss police receive great assistance in their duties from the rest of the populace, making the effective police force over seven million strong. Once a Swiss starts obeying the myriad laws, he is inclined to think all his fellow countrymen should also obey them. Unlike in the UK where 'cheating the system' is applauded, the Swiss see the point of minor legislation and so help enforce it. If you have just paid 5 francs (£2) for a year's compulsory cycle insurance, you are going to be unhappy letting others pedal about for free. Thus seemingly unenforceable statutes such as not washing cars on a Sunday or having a garden bonfire on any day of the week but Saturday, are easily policed by the 'net curtain brigade' who have no hesitation in reporting offenders.

More tax evaders are brought to book by tip-offs from the public than from the tax authorities' own investigations. Traditionally Swiss crime has been of a financial nature, corrupt officials taking back-handers, savers being swindled in pyramid investment scams, and money laundering (although it is unclear if the latter really is a crime in Switzerland).

By international standards crime in Switzerland is low. Recent figures also show that nearly 45% of offences are committed by a small but highly efficient criminal element among the foreign contingent (who else?).

Despite low crime, Swiss prisons are always full. Voters approved a plan to build more and within days of completion the new prisons were full too. It does not seem to occur to the Swiss that there could be a correlation between overcrowding and the fact that their prisons are roughly equivalent to a good three-star hotel.

Much of the recent increase in crime is drug related:

either dealers fighting over their patch, or addicts stealing bicycles to support their habit. Over 80,000 are stolen a year – it's a hopeless cycle.

The Swiss police are a dowdy lot. In their grey uniforms, they can easily be mistaken for postmen, but postmen do not usually carry guns, except when going to compulsory army shooting practice. They also have an alarming tendency to break out the tear gas and rubber bullets at the drop of a helmet. Many a demonstration is brought to a tearful conclusion in this way, but it provokes little or no comment.

Much police revenue comes from fining anything that moves too fast or stops too long (or does either correctly but in the wrong place). Another revenue raiser is the issuing of forms, at 15 to 20 francs a time, to innocent people to confirm their innocence. In order to work for the government, or stand a better chance of being accepted as a tenant for an apartment, or simply hang on the wall, certificates are available from the police declaring that the holder has no criminal record, or at least has not yet been caught.

# Language

A linguistic map of Switzerland would indicate that the majority of the people speak German. This is not true. The spoken language or dialect of the majority of Swiss is Swiss-German which is known as *Schwizerdütsch*, or *Schwüzertüütsch*, or *Schwyzertütsch*, etc. No two Swiss are able to agree on its spelling, but it does not matter because it is not a written language. Nor is it uniform. Each town has its own version. There is *Baseldytsch*, *Berndütsch*, *Bündnerdütsch*, *Züridütsch* – the list is roughly equivalent to the number of valleys.

To write, the Swiss-German-speaking Swiss use High German, known rather tellingly as *Schriftdeutsch*, i.e., 'written German'.

There are even some differences between Swiss-style High German and the Germans' German, rather like the difference between American and British English. Americans call a tram a street car; Germans call it a *Strassenbahn*; the Swiss call a tram a *Tram*. Many words are regarded as too German and alternatives are used. *Urlaub*, the German for holiday, does not sound like much of a holiday to the Swiss, so they go on *Ferien* instead. In order to trip up Germans in their own tongue, the Swiss obstinately introduce their own words and versions of German. The Lake of Zurich should be called by the logic of the German language the *Züricher See* and many visiting Germans fall into this trap if not the lake itself. The Swiss call it the *Zürichsee*.

*Danke*, thanks, is often regarded as too German, so the Swiss-Germans say *Merci*. To avoid being mistaken for French-speakers they add 'very much' in German. But to avoid being mistaken for Germans who started a phrase in French and forgot the rest, it is not the High German *vielmals*, but the Swiss-German version without an 's'. The result is very odd, very bilingual and very Swiss: *merci vielmal*.

## Divided by a Common Tongue

Having one's own dialect is the ultimate regional divider. Federations of states like the USA are all very well, but it is not until you can identify your fellow countryman as a foreigner when he opens his mouth that it really becomes fun.

To Swiss ears, the various versions of Swiss-German dialects range from cute to painful (their own dialect being, of course, perfect). To the English-speaker, they all sound painful. Swiss-German is an old guttural farmers' tongue that incorporates many throat-clearing sounds, hardly the language for nice young ladies. But, despite nice young ladies, throat-dependent Swiss-German is as strong as ever and in no danger of dying out.

Television and radio in the German-speaking areas are conducted almost exclusively in Swiss-German. The advent of local TV stations has even brought the news in Swiss-German – though how they read an unwritten language remains a mystery.

Swiss-German has not given the world much besides *muesli* and *Rösti*, and it has kept its proverbs and sayings to itself. Many of these reflect Switzerland's odd mix of farming and high finance. 'As dark as in a cow' comes from the farm. While 'Speaking is silver, to be silent is gold' originates somewhere near the stock exchange. Before starting work each day Swiss dentists chant 'The morning hour has gold in its mouth'.

With four official languages (German, French, Italian and Romansh), things can get complicated. Swiss milk cartons are so cluttered with multi-lingual instructions about storing at 3-5°C and details of the mineral content, that they hardly have any space to show a cow.

From the back of the word-packed cornflakes packet at the breakfast table onwards, Swiss children are brought up in a linguistic blender. In addition to their own tongue, youngsters learn a second Swiss national language at school. But it is the plight of Swiss-German-speaking children (brought up speaking *Schwizerdütsch)* to have to master High German (for reading and writing), before they can learn any other.

Significantly, warnings at stations not to cross the rails are in German, French, Italian as well as English. They only need be in English, as no Swiss would ever be daft enough to cross the rails.

# Oh to be in English

The English language is popular and extremely fashionable in Switzerland – even the graffiti are sprayed in it. All Swiss speak English, from Arosa, whose publicity slogan is 'Just 4 You', to Zurich – 'The Little Big City'.

English in Switzerland comes in many forms. There is 'Swinglish' – half Swiss, half English. These are words that the Swiss are convinced are used in everyday English, like a 'smoking' for a dinner jacket or tuxedo. A track suit is called a 'trainer' which in English is either a person who coaches a sports team or half a pair of running shoes. Switzerland is covered in green plastic-bag dispensers for dog owners to put their pooch's poo in (which proves that if they can get dog owners to do this, nothing is impossible). The name of these dispensers is 'Robidog' (half Robocop, half a cop out), since none of the Swiss languages was deemed suitable. Even the curse of modern times, the mobile phone, is dubbed the 'handy'.

Swinglish should not be mistaken for the real English that is thrown into most sentences Swiss people utter. Words like 'know-how', 'insider tip', 'ticket', 'meeting' and 'fixer'. In recent years 'sorry' has even replaced *es tut mir leid* on the rare occasions when the Swiss-Germans have to apologise.

The use of English is taken to extreme lengths in advertising. Posters and commercials implore the Swiss to 'Take it easy', 'Get the Feeling', join 'Das Dream Team' engage in 'Safer Sex' and, falling back into Swinglish, tell them 'it's Pretty Woman'. Even the official road safety campaign posters state simply in English 'No Drinks, No Drugs, No Problems'.

# The Author

Born in Southport, Lancashire, Paul Bilton recently became what is known somewhat unaffectionately as a 'paper Swiss'. (First marry a Swiss, then live in the country for five years, fill in forms, wait another 18 months, and finally hand over several hundred Swiss francs in cash for the paper which grants you Swiss nationality to the local postman when he delivers your mail.)

A short career in magazine publishing was preceded by an even shorter career in advertising ('Ferguson's Fertilizers Fertilize Faster'). In the 1980s he launched a business to manufacture plastic products under his own patent, and later left both the business and Britain to become an *Ausländer* in Switzerland.

His book *The Perpetual Tourist – in search of a Swiss role* is published by Bergli Books of Basel, and between writing, broadcasting and giving talks about Swiss life, he gives odd English lessons. He tries hard to worry more, but still cannot understand why it is frowned upon to redecorate his nuclear shelter himself.

He and his Swiss wife live an idyllic life by the Zurich lake-shore where he collects coffee creamer tops while she embroiders car cushions. They enjoy a near perfect diet of *muesli* and *Rösti*, but never on the same plate.

---